CAJUN DANCE HALL Special

FIDDLE EDITION

A cassette tape and compact disc of the music in this book are now available. The publisher strongly recommends the use of one of these recordings along with the text to insure accuracy of interpretation and ease in learning.

IN CONJUNCTION WITH ROUNDER RECORDS

ROUNDER

CONTENTS

INTRODUCTION

During the past twenty years, Cajun music has experienced a joyful renaissance at home while also reaching broad new global audiences. Along with other committed companies like Swallow, Arhoolie, and La Louisianne, Rounder Records has helped bolster this resurgence with an energetic recording campaign. *Cajun Dance Hall Special* culls more highlights from Rounder's Louisiana releases, presenting a diverse array of Cajun styles and stylists.

The first piquant performer here [as performed on the accompanying recording] is accordionist Bruce Daigrepont. In addition to his agile playing and impassioned vocals, Daigrepont is one of Cajun music's most prolific and articulate young songwriters, as evidenced by "Coeur des Cajuns" and "Arc en ciel." The latter song features fine twin fiddling by Waylon Thibodeaux and Gina Forsythe. Belton Richard's swamp-pop ballad "Un autre soir ennuyant" spotlights Sue Daigrepont on piano; another notable accompanist is ace drummer Kenny Blevins, whose prestigious resume includes work with John Hiatt, Sonny Landreth, Snooks Eaglin, and L'il Queenie and the Percolators.

Jo-El Sonnier's diverse roots-music mastery invites comparison with Ray Charles and Lonnie Mack. Equally adept at Cajun tunes, country music, blues, swamp-pop and rock, Sonnier has emerged lately as a commercial-country chart-topper. He was raised on traditional Cajun music, however, and concentrates here on stunning renditions of such standards as "Les flammes d'enfer" ("the Flames of Hell.") Besides his sparing vocals, Sonnier also plays a mean squeeze-box.

Since grouping together in 1988, Steve Riley and the Mamou Playboys have quickly become Cajun music's most popular young traditional band. Their unvarnished sound honors the concepts of such mentors as the late Dewey Balfa, yet also includes innovations like the harmony vocals on "La pointe aux pins." Only twenty-three at this writing, Steve Riley is already a formidable accordionist. His prodigious talent is matched by David Greely's supple fiddling, and the solid-yet-subtle rhythm section of guitarist Kevin Barzas, drummer Mike "Chop" Chapman, and percussionist Christine Balfa. Beyond their cultural significance, the Mamou Playboys are a red-hot dance band, as heard here on the lively instrumental "High Point Two-Step."

Jimmy C. Newman is best known for the mid-'70s hit "Lache pas la patate," ("Don't Drop the Potato"), a message song about perseverance. For nearly forty years, though, Newman has served as Cajun music's leading link with country music, and a mainstay of the Grand Ole Opry. He appears here in an atypically mainstream Cajun setting, and rises to the occasion with powerful, poignant vocals on "J'aurais du t'aimer" and "La bague que brille." Newman's aptly-named band, Cajun Country, gets an instrumental work-out on the upbeat "La 'tit cord," with inspired solos by accordionist Bessyl Duhon and fiddler Rufus Thibodeaux.

Fiddler Michael Doucet is a pivotal figure in the Cajun music renaissance. Doucet's trailblazing style blends a scholarly knowledge of Cajun folk-tradition with an adventurous penchant for rock, jazz and points beyond. This eclectic approach was first expressed in a band known as Coteau. Today Doucet's main vehicle is the progressive band Beausoleil, along with loosely-formed groups like Cajun Brew. The adrenalized "Rolling Pin" offers a crash course in cutting-edge Cajun music, while Doucet's solo on "Valse bébé takes harmonic tangents which are well past the parameters of traditional Cajun fiddling.

Beausoleil's uniqueness is also forged by guitarist David Doucet, who has encircled Cajun music with Appalachian finger-picking in the Doc Watson mode. Doucet's deft execution of this difficult synthesis graces all of Beausoleil's tracks here, and is also the focus of "Balfa Waltz," "Ton Papa," and "T'en as eu," from his solo album *Quand J'ai Parti*. In addition, these songs showcase David Doucet as a forceful and convincing singer.

Accordionist Eddie LeJeune is one of the most ethnic stylists in contemporary Cajun music. The raw soul of "Grande Bosco" and "Dans la porte je suis après espérer" represent the legacy of his father, Iry, who is revered as one of Cajun music's best singers, accordionists, and songwriters. (The late Iry LeJeune's work is available on the Goldband label out of Lake Charles, Louisiana, and should not be missed.) Eddie LeJeune's performances here come from two different sessions. Featured accompanists include fiddler and fiddle-maker Lionel LeLeux, and guitarist D.L. Menard, who shines here as an impeccable one-man rhythm section.

Menard is prominent in his own right, of course, as both an expressive singer and the writer of such modern classics as "La porte d'en arrière." In fact, Menard's succinct eloquence has earned him the nickname "the Cajun Hank Williams." "The Water Pump" is an original admonition to not take loved ones for granted, echoing the folk wisdom of the ubiquitous lyric "you don't miss your water 'til your well runs dry." Menard's expressive singing gives Lawrence Walker's "Little Black Eyes" an especially heartfelt rendering.

Like Michael Doucet, Zachary Richard was a pioneer in the cultural consciousness-raising which helped revive Cajun music. An accordionist, songwriter and powerful vocalist, Richard made many of his activist statements in a rock-and-roll context, and his extroverted stage presence has inspired the moniker "the Cajun Mick Jagger." The prolific Richard remains hugely popular in both South Louisiana and Quebec, and is currently moving in major-label rock circles. He is in excellent voice here on both a hard-rocking arrangement of the traditional "Bayou Pon Pon," and a swinging version of "Jolie blon."

This anthology presents a thorough cross-section of today's contemporary Cajun styles. From unadorned ethnic sounds to the most futuristic concepts, the spectrum includes plenty of straight-ahead dancehall favorites, and also shows the influence of country music, swamp-pop and rock. What's more, each song here represents a fine album with plenty more great material. Such diverse quality is yet another good omen for the healthy future of Cajun music.

—Ben Sandmel
[Ben Sandmel is a New Orleans based drummer, and a
journalist and folklore researcher whose articles
have appeared in The *Atlantic*, *Esquire* and *The Chicago Sun-Times*.]

COEUR DES CAJUNS

LES GRANDS BOIS

LA POINTE AUX PINS

J'AURAIS DU T'AIMER

ROLLING PIN

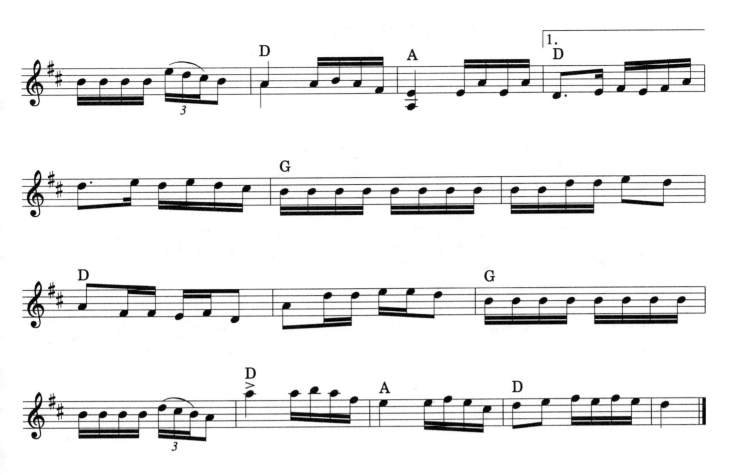

BALFA WALTZ

GRANDE BOSCO

ALLONS À LAFAYETTE

ARC EN CIEL

20

LIKE A REAL CAJUN

25

LA BAGUE QUE BRILLE

*This page has been
left blank to avoid
awkward page turns*

HIGH POINTE 2 STEP

28

LITTLE BLACK EYES

T'EN AS EU

UN AUTRE SOIR ENNUYANT

*This page has been
left blank to avoid
awkward page turns*

BAYOU PON PON

VALSE BÉBÉ

THE WATER PUMP

TON PAPA

LA'TIT CORD

1) Accordion
2) Dobro

Accordion

Fiddle *D. S.* %

DANS LA PORTE JE SUIS APRÉS ESPÉRER

J'AI PASSÉ DEVANT TA PORTE

JOLIE BLON

LES FLAMMES D' ENFER

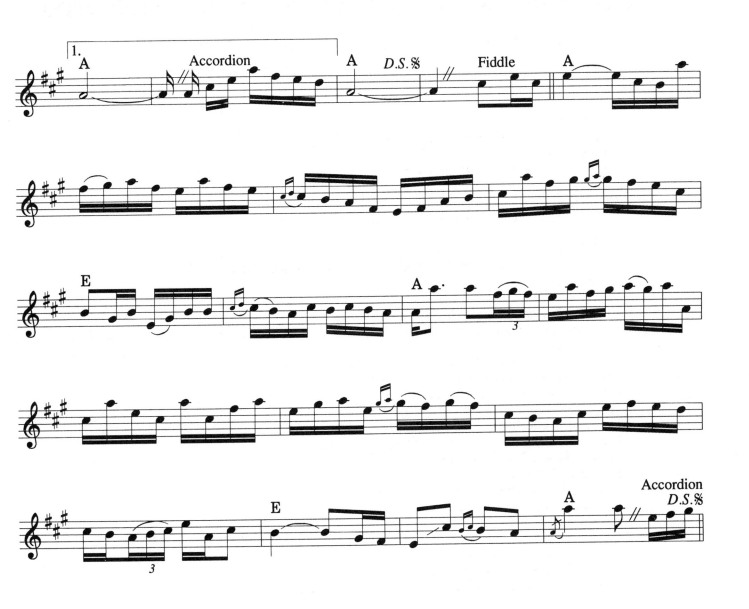

These recordings and many others are available from

Round-Up Records, 1 Camp St. Cambridge MA 02140.

To order with Visa or Master Card call 1-800-44-DISCS.

Ricky Skaggs can be heard on:
J. D. Crowe and the New South (Rounder 0044)
Boone Creek (Rounder 0081) Cassette only
Ricky Skaggs **Family and Friends**

Brad Leftwich can be heard on:
Bob Carlin Bangin' & Sawin' (Rounder 0197) cassette only

J. P. Fraley can be heard on:
J. P. and Annadeene Fraley **Wild Rose of the Mountain** (Rounder 0037)
cassette only

Scotty Stoneman can be heard on:
The Kentucky Colonels **1965 - 1967** (Rounder 0070) cassette only

Eddie Stubbs can be heard with the Johnson Mountain Boys on:
The Johnson Mountain Boys (Rounder 0135) cassette only
Walls of Time (Rounder 0160) Cassette only
Working Close (Rounder 0185) cassette only
Live at the Birchmere (Rounder 0191)
We'll Still Sing On (Rounder 0205) cassette only
Let the Whole World Talk (Rounder 0225)
Requests (Rounder 0246)
At the Old Schoolhouse (Rounder 0260/61)
Blue Diamond (Rounder 0293)
Favorites (Rounder 11509)

James Bryan can be heard on:
James Bryan **The First of May** (Rounder 0215) cassette only
James Bryan **Lookout Blues** (Rounder 0207) cassette only

Vassar Clements can be heard on:
Vassar Clements **Grass Routes** (Rounder 0287)
Hartford, Clements & Holland (Rounder 0207)

Alison Krauss can be heard on:
Alison Krauss **Too Late to Cry** (Rounder 0235)
Alison Krauss and Union Station **Two Highways** (Rounder 0265)
Alison Krauss **I've Got That Old Feeling** (Rounder 0275)
Alison Krauss and Union Station **Everytime You Say Goodbye** (Rounder 0285)

Sam Bush can be heard on:
Sam Bush **Late As Usual** (Rounder 0195)

Richard Green can be heard on:
Richard Green **Ramblin'** (Rounder 0110)

Mark O'Connor can be heard on:
Mark O'Connor (Rounder 0046) cassette only
Mark O'Connor **Pickin' In the Wind** (Rounder 0068) cassette only
Mark O'Connor **Markology** (Rounder 0090)
Mark O'Connor **On the Rampage** (Rounder 0118) cassette only
Mark O'Connor **Soppin' the Gravy** (Rounder 0137)
Mark O'Connor **False Dawn** (Rounder 02165) cassette only
Mark O'Connor **Retrospective** (Rounder 11507) CD only

Norman and Nancy Blake can be heard on:
Norman and Nancy Blake **Blind Dog** (Rounder 0254)
The Norman and Nancy Blake Compact Disc (Rounder 11505) CD only
Norman and Nancy Blake **Natasha's Waltz** (Rounder 11530) CD only

Blaine Sprouse and *Kenny Baker* can be heard on:
Blaine Sprouse and Kenny Baker **Indian Springs** (Rounder 0259)
Blaine Sprouse **Summertime** (Rounder 0155) cassette only
Blaine Sprouse **Brilliancy** (Rounder 0209) cassette only

Bobby Hicks can be heard with the Bluegrass Album Band on:
The Bluegrass Album (Rounder 0140)
The Bluegrass Album Volume 2 (Rounder 0164)
The Bluegrass Album Volume 3 (Rounder 0180)
The Bluegrass Album Volume 4 (Rounder 0210)
The Bluegrass Album Volume 5 (Rounder 0240)
The Bluegrass Album Compact Disc (Rounder 11502) CD only
The Bluegrass Album Compact Disc Volume 2 (Rounder 11516) CD only

Byron Berline can be heard on:
Byron Berline **Dad's Favorites** (Rounder 0100)

Stuart Duncan can be heard on:
Stuart Duncan (Rounder 0263)
The Nashville Bluegrass Band **My Native Home** (Rounder 0212)
The Nashville Bluegrass Band **Idle Time** (Rounder 0232)
The Nashville Bluegrass Band **To Be His Child** (Rounder 0242)

Tony Rice can be heard on:
Tony Rice (Rounder 0085)
Tony Rice **Manzanita** (Rounder 0092)
Tony Rice **Cold On the Shoulder** (Rounder 0183)
Tony Rice **Me & My Guitar** (Rounder 0201)
Norman Blake & Tony Rice **Blake and Rice** (Rounder 0233)
Tony Rice **Native American** (Rounder 0248)
Tony Rice Plays and Sings Bluegrass (Rounder 0253)
The Rice **Brothers** (Rounder 0256)
Norman Blake & Tony Rice 2 (Rounder 0266)
Tony Rice **Acoustics** (Rounder 0317)
Tony Rice Unit **Mar West** (Rounder 0125) cassette only
Tony Rice Unit **Still Inside** (Rounder 0150) cassette only
Tony Rice Unit **Backwaters** (Rounder 0167)
Tony Rice Unit **Devlin** (Rounder 11531) CD only

Russ Barenberg can be heard on:
Russ Barenberg **Cowboy Calypso** (Rounder 0111) cassette only
Russ Barenberg **Man Behind the Melodies** (Rounder 0176) cassette only
Russ Barenberg **Moving Pictures** (Rounder 0249)
Russ Barenberg **Halloween Rehearsal** (Rounder 11534) CD only

Artie Traum can be heard on:
Artie Traum Cayenne (Rounder 3084)

Guy Van Duser can be heard on:
Guy Van Duser **Finger Style Guitar Solos** (Rounder 3021) cassette only
Guy Van Duser **Stride Guitar** (Rounder 3059) cassette only
Guy Van Duser **I've Got the World On a String** (Rounder 3081) cassette only
and Guy Van Duser **American Finger Style Guitar** (Rounder 11533) CD only